SHE WAS THE FIRST!

THE TRAILBLAZING LIFE OF SHIRLEY CHISHOLM

BY KATHERYN RUSSELL-BROWN

ILLUSTRATIONS BY ERIC VELASQUEZ

Lee & Low Books Inc.   New York

ACKNOWLEDGMENTS

Thank-you to the following people for their generous help with this book: Barbara Winslow, Professor Emerita, Brooklyn College and Founder/Director Emerita of the Shirley Chisholm Project of Brooklyn Women's Activism; Patty Lamiell, Director of Media Relations, Teachers College, Columbia University; Nissa Marie Koerner, Press Secretary, Office of Congresswoman Barbara Lee; and Colleen Bradley-Sanders, Associate Professor and College Archivist, and Marianne LaBatto, Associate Archivist, Brooklyn College Library Archives and Special Collections.

Edited by Louise E. May
Designed by Christy Hale
Production by The Kids at Our House
The text is set in Bulmer
The illustrations are rendered in watercolor
Manufactured in China by Toppan
Printed on paper from responsible sources
10 9 8 7 6 5 4 3 2 1
First Edition

Library of Congress Cataloging-in-Publication Data
Names: Russell-Brown, Katheryn, 1961- author. | Velasquez, Eric, illustrator.
Title: She was the first! : the trailblazing life of Shirley Chisholm / by Katheryn Russell-Brown ; illustrations by Eric Velasquez.
Description: First edition. | New York : Lee & Low Books, 2020. | Includes bibliographical references. | Summary: "A picture biography of educator and politician Shirley Chisholm, who in 1968 was the first Black woman elected to Congress and in 1972 was the first Black candidate from a major political party (the Democratic party) to run for the United States presidency. An afterword with additional information, photographs, and source lists are included"—Provided by publisher.
Identifiers: LCCN 2019029618 | ISBN 9781620143469 (hardcover)
Subjects: LCSH: Chisholm, Shirley, 1924-2005—Biography—Juvenile literature. | African American legislators—Biography—Juvenile literature. | Women legislators—United States—Biography—Juvenile literature. | African American teachers—Biography—Juvenile literature. | Teachers—United States—Biography—Juvenile literature.
Classification: LCC E840.8.C48 R87 2020 | DDC 328.73/092 [B]—dc23
LC record available at https://lccn.loc.gov/2019029618

To anyone who's dreamed of doing something that other people say is silly or impossible—go ahead and try. Create your own path and be a trailblazer, like Shirley Chisholm.

—K.R.-B.

For Shirley Chisholm, and the often overlooked people of the West Indian community who have made valuable contributions to American history and culture.   —E.V.

On a cold November day in 1924, Shirley Anita St. Hill came into this world. Back then, nobody had an inkling that she would open a door to history.

Shirley, the oldest of the St. Hill girls, was a handful for Mother

and Papa. From the time she was little, Shirley liked to be in charge.
At three, she was already leading children twice her age around the
neighborhood, telling them where to go and which games to play.

"Listen to me!" Shirley said. And they did.

The St. Hill family lived in Brooklyn, New York. Papa was a baker's helper, and Mother was a seamstress and domestic worker. They barely earned enough money to keep food in the cupboards and supper on the table.

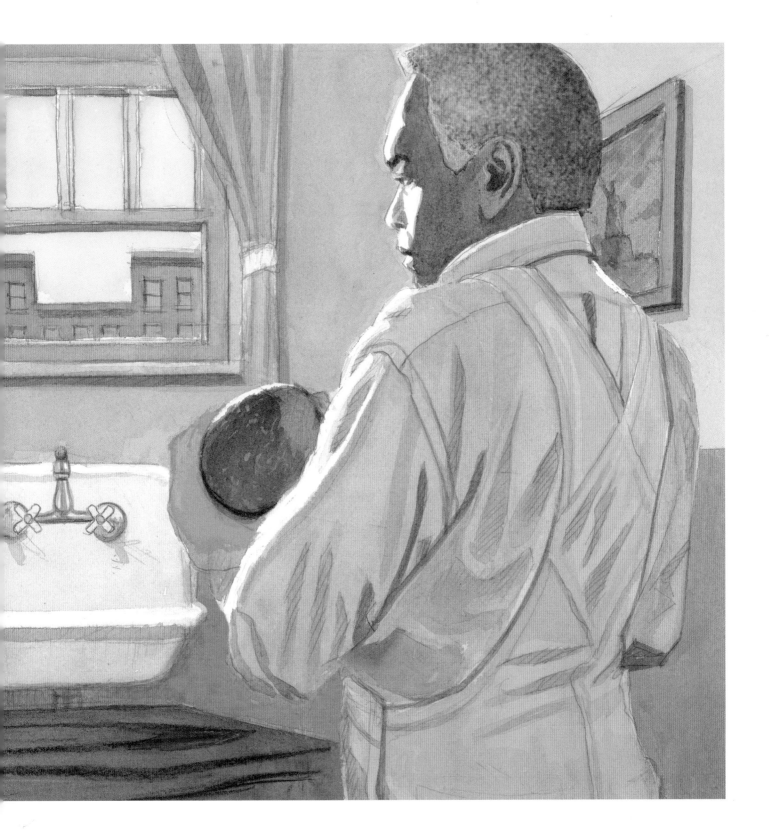

Mother and Papa made a tough decision. They would send the girls
to live with Mother's family on the Caribbean island of Barbados. While
the children were away, Papa and Mother would save their money, and
Shirley and her sisters would get a taste of country living.

In 1928, Shirley, her sisters, and Mother boarded an ocean liner named the *Vulcania*. After nine rocky days at sea, they arrived in Barbados.

From the port they rode a rickety bus to Grandmother Emmeline's farm. Shirley spotted her grandmother right away. The thin West Indian woman stood as tall as a reed, and she looked like serious business.

Island life was nothing like city living. The days were as hot as an oven
and every night Shirley heard an animal concert of chirps, clucks, and moos.
Her new home also had something Shirley had never seen: an outhouse!

Mother stayed for a few months to make sure the girls were settled in.

Then she had to go back to Brooklyn to help Papa.

The day Mother left everyone's face was wet with tears.

Grandmother Emmeline's house was stocked with love, rules, and chores.

Fetch the well water.

Feed the animals.

Graze the cows.

When they finished, Shirley, her sisters, and her cousins enjoyed a special treat. They raced to the beach, ran through the sand, and jumped into the clear blue water. To Shirley, the ocean water felt like warm magic.

The local school was a one-room building with more than a hundred children ages four to eleven. The teachers were strict and punished students who did not behave.

Shirley was a fast learner. She could read and write before she turned five.

Barbados was filled with people with brown skin like Shirley's. She saw teachers, preachers, and shopkeepers taking care of island business. Seeing them, Shirley understood that when she grew up, she could take charge and get things done too.

Seven years went by. Mother and Papa were still struggling to earn
money. The Great Depression of the 1930s made it hard for them to
find steady jobs. But no matter. Mother wanted her girls back home.
In 1934, the year Shirley turned ten, she and her sisters moved

back to Brooklyn and a different life. The city was crowded with
automobiles, tall buildings, fast-moving people, and a confusing maze
of streets. During the icicle-cold winters, Shirley shivered thinking
about the warm Barbados sunshine.

At her new school, Shirley got a sad surprise. Instead of starting sixth grade, she was put back into fourth grade. Shirley's schooling in Barbados had been excellent, but the teachers in Brooklyn said she didn't know enough US history.

Shirley was upset and embarrassed. And bored. Sometimes when the teacher wasn't looking, Shirley threw spitballs and snapped rubber bands at the younger kids in her class.

Once her teacher realized why Shirley misbehaved, the school gave her a tutor. In time, Shirley learned all the history she needed to catch up with her classmates.

Education was important in the St. Hill home. The girls made regular trips to the library to borrow books. When holidays came, Shirley was sure to receive a book as a present.

Every evening the family dinner table came alive. Papa talked first. Shirley listened closely and asked questions as he discussed world events. Papa read three newspapers every day. He was full of information.

When Papa's friends stopped by, Shirley stayed up late and listened through the bedroom door. The men talked for hours about world leaders and politics. Papa said everybody should be treated the same—poor, rich, Black, White.

Papa's words stirred something inside Shirley. She started paying more attention to current events.

In high school, Shirley earned top grades and was accepted at several colleges. She chose Brooklyn College, just a subway ride away from home. The school was bigger than any she had attended. There were so many students!

Shirley loved her classes. Her brain buzzed with new information about other countries, foreign languages, and different cultures. She joined the

Harriet Tubman Society, a club where she learned more about Black history. And nobody was surprised when Shirley signed up for the debate team. She could outtalk anybody.

After her schoolwork was done, Shirley enjoyed going to parties and dancing.

Shirley wanted to use her education to make the country and the world better for everyone. But how? Her favorite teacher, Professor Warsoff, knew Shirley was a great debater. He suggested she give politics a try.

Shirley had doubts. She loved children, so she decided to be a schoolteacher instead of a politician. She would make a difference by helping children.

After she finished college in 1946, Shirley had a hard time finding a job. Most doors were closed to her because she was Black and she was a woman. Plus, she was very short!

"Don't judge me by my size," Shirley insisted at an interview to be a nursery school teacher. "Give me a chance!"

Shirley got the job.

During the day, Shirley worked with children. In the evenings, she worked with community groups.

Shirley noticed that people with power and money didn't seem to care about folks who were poor. This bothered her. She remembered how it felt to be poor. So she spoke up and tried to make a difference for people who didn't have power or money.

One time Shirley encouraged the women in a local group to stand up to the men and demand respect. Another time she noticed that the officials in charge of a meeting were ignoring everyone waiting in line to ask questions. Shirley rushed to the front and made sure that everyone was allowed to talk.

In the middle of all this work, Shirley found love. In 1949, she married Conrad Chisholm, a private investigator. He was handsome, smart, and crazy about Shirley.

In the 1950s and '60s, Shirley joined many organizations. Some local leaders and politicians didn't like her ideas. They called her a troublemaker because she stood up for women and people of color. But the people who needed help were glad Shirley was on their side, fighting to make sure they were treated fairly.

By 1964, Shirley's heart told her it was time to step into politics. She had a gift. People listened when she talked. Her words motivated them to action.

Shirley decided to take a chance and run for the New York State Assembly.

She won!

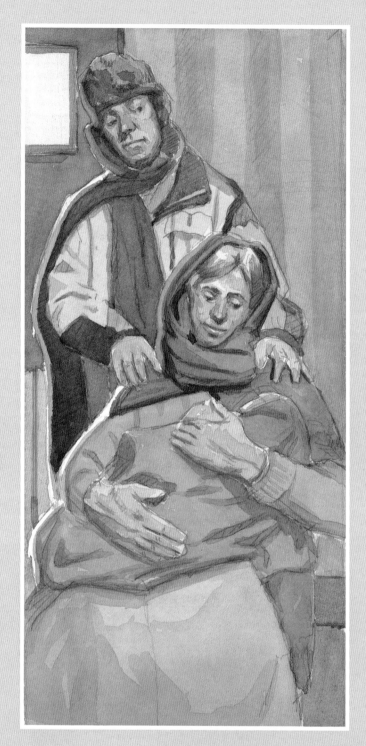

After Shirley became an assemblywoman, she worked to help the people of New York.

She worked to pass laws to help sick people get the medicine they needed.

She worked to make sure landlords kept the heat on in the winter.

She worked to help people find jobs and to raise pay for workers,

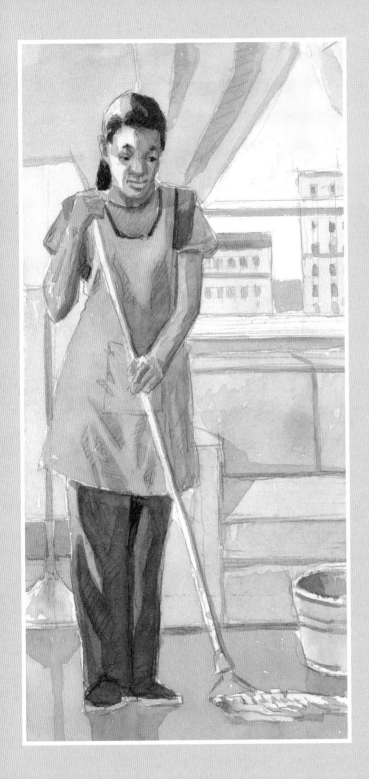

including those who cleaned houses like her mother.

She worked to help poor students pay for college.

Shirley didn't say or do things just to be popular. She fought for what she believed was right, not what was easy. She followed Grandmother Emmeline's advice always to speak the truth.

Four years later, Shirley decided to run for the US Congress. She promised to help people all across the country.

Some of the men in Congress tried to keep Shirley out. They scolded her and said that women didn't belong in politics. One of her opponents called her a "little schoolteacher." Many people said they would never vote for a woman.

Shirley dusted off the mean talk. She kept meeting with people and asking them to vote for her. Her campaign slogan was "Unbought and Unbossed."

Shirley's hard work paid off. In 1968, she was the first Black woman elected to Congress. In the House of Representatives, Shirley kept her promise. She worked for laws that helped women, children, students, poor people, farmworkers, Native people, and others who were often pushed aside. She fought for healthcare. She spoke up for military veterans. She spoke out against war.

BRING U.S. TOGETHER

VOTE **CHISHOLM** 1972
UNBOUGHT AND UNBOSSED

While in Congress, Shirley gave many speeches, and people of every color and background liked her ideas for change. But Shirley wanted to take her message to an even bigger audience. So in 1972, she decided to seek the highest political office in the United States. Shirley was the first Black person, Democrat or Republican, to run for president.

Shirley's campaign was full of ups and downs. Although many people helped her and followed the "Chisholm Trail," their support wasn't enough. Shirley didn't win the nomination, but her work paved the way for the future—for the first Black president of the United States and one day the first woman president.

Shirley Anita St. Hill Chisholm opened a door to history!

AFTERWORD

SHIRLEY ANITA ST. HILL was born on November 30, 1924, in Brooklyn, New York. Her parents, Charles St. Hill and Ruby Seale St. Hill, emigrated to the United States from Barbados. Shirley's mother was a religious woman. She took her daughters to church three times every Sunday. Shirley's father, a voracious reader and a devoted follower of the Black nationalist leader Marcus Garvey, passed along his love of politics, race relations, and history to Shirley.

With the goal of saving money and exposing their children to Caribbean life, the St. Hills sent them to live for a time in Barbados. The three girls—Shirley, age three; Odessa, age two; and Muriel, eight months—stayed with their maternal grandmother, Emmeline Seale. They lived on her farm from 1928 to 1934. Describing life at her grandmother's house, Shirley said, "The furniture was sparse and plain, but we found Grandmother's house elaborately furnished with the two necessities: warmth and love." Shirley's education in Barbados's British-style schools was traditional and strict, and it gave Shirley a solid foundation in speaking and writing. Punishment, however, could be severe, and the teachers sometimes flogged children, including Shirley, for not paying attention in class.

In March 1934, when the girls returned to Brooklyn, Shirley discovered that she had a new little sister, Selma. The family's economic fortunes had not improved. The Great Depression had taken hold, and Shirley saw her parents struggle to make ends meet.

Shirley excelled in school. In high school she studied French and won an achievement award. She was also elected vice president of Junior Arista, an honor society. She received several college scholarships and had her heart set on attending Vassar College in upstate New

RIGHT: Shirley St. Hill senior yearbook picture, Brooklyn College, 1946

York or Oberlin College in Ohio. However, Shirley's parents made it clear that they could not afford the room-and-board expenses at those schools. So Shirley stayed at home and attended Brooklyn College. She majored in sociology and minored in Spanish. She joined the Harriet Tubman Society, where members had discussions about Black racial consciousness and racism in American society. During this time, Shirley became concerned about issues surrounding discrimination in hiring, working conditions, pay, and advancement opportunities for Blacks and women. She was also active on the debate team. Her star matches drew the attention of Louis Warsoff, a blind, White political science professor. He strongly encouraged Shirley to pursue politics.

In 1946, Shirley graduated from college cum laude. Teaching was one of the few professional doors open to young Black women at that time. Shirley loved children and felt she could be of service to society by pursuing a career in education. Her first job

was as a nursery school teacher at Mt. Calvary Child Care Center in Harlem. She also earned a master's degree in curriculum and teaching from Teachers College, Columbia University in 1951 and later became director of the Child Care Center of Hamilton-Madison House on Manhattan's Lower East Side. From 1959 to 1964, she served as a consultant to the New York City Division of Daycare.

During her time as an educator, Shirley Chisholm also maintained an active political agenda. She joined the New York State Seventeenth Assembly District Democratic Club, a local political club, and was involved in numerous groups that addressed community concerns, including the National Association for the Advancement of Colored People (NAACP) and the Urban League.

Beyond being a founding member of several organizations, including the National Organization for Women (NOW) and the Congressional Black Caucus, Chisholm was a woman of many other firsts. In 1964, she was the first Black woman elected to the New York State Assembly. In 1968, she was the first Black woman elected to the US Congress. She held her seat in the House of Representatives for seven terms (fourteen years). In 1972, she was the first Black candidate from a major political party to run for the US presidency. At the same time, she

ABOVE: Congresswoman Shirley Chisholm opening her presidential campaign in Cambridge, Massachusetts, February 15, 1972

LEFT: Presidential campaign button

was the first woman and first Black person in the Democratic Party to seek that office. Chisholm received more than 430,000 votes in the primary and earned 152 delegates.

Chisholm's runs for political office were not easy. She was a no-nonsense politician. Her small stature combined with her fiery and dynamic presentation often surprised people. She had a multiracial coalition of supporters and fans around the world. She worked to increase spending for education and healthcare. However, as a Black woman, Chisholm encountered both anti-woman and anti-Black backlash. Some Black men did not support her because she was a woman. Many people thought a Black man should be the first person of color to run for the presidency. White male politicians expected Chisholm to step aside. They questioned her womanhood and her race loyalty. Although these criticisms stung, Chisholm refused to be placed in a box.

She was a political trailblazer who said, "I am the candidate of the people . . . who dared to be a catalyst of change."

In 1983, Chisholm retired from Congress. She cofounded the National [Political] Congress of Black Women in 1984 and supported Rev. Jesse Jackson's presidential campaigns in 1984 and 1988. She was a popular speaker on the lecture circuit and taught at Mount Holyoke College. Another part of her work was to document her personal story. She wrote two books, *Unbought and Unbossed* (1970) and *The Good Fight* (1973). She was a mentor to many up-and-coming Black women politicians, most notably Congresswoman Barbara Lee, a Democrat from California. Chisholm also served as a role model for many other politicians across race and gender lines.

Shirley was married to Conrad Chisholm from 1949 to 1977. Following

RIGHT: Shirley Chisholm and Rev. Jesse Jackson at a news conference in Atlanta, Georgia, 1985

their divorce, she married Arthur Hardwick later that year. They were married until his death in 1986. On January 1, 2005, Shirley Anita St. Hill Chisholm passed away in Ormond Beach, Florida.

Chisholm's alma mater, Brooklyn College, is home to the Shirley Chisholm Project, dedicated to bringing her life and legacy to the general public. The project also hosts an annual Shirley Chisholm Day on November 30, her birthday. In 2014, Chisholm was honored with a US postage stamp, and in 2015, she was posthumously awarded the Presidential Medal of Freedom by President Barack Obama, the first Black president of the United States. In 2019, Shirley Chisholm State Park opened in Brooklyn, and in 2020, a statue of Chisholm was erected at an entrance to Brooklyn's Prospect Park. It is one of only a few statues in New York City that honors a woman or person of color.

ABOVE: Shirley Chisholm and Barbara Lee at an event in Berkeley, California, 1995; Lee has served in Congress since 1998

RIGHT: Entrance to the new Shirley Chisholm State Park in Brooklyn, New York, June 4, 2019

QUOTATION SOURCES

page 5: "Listen to me!" Chisholm, quoted in "Shirley Chisholm, 'Unbossed' Pioneer in Congress, Is Dead at 80." *New York Times* obituary.

page 25: "Don't judge . . . my size," Chisholm, *Unbought and Unbossed* (40th Anniversary Edition), p. 45.

"Give me a chance!" Ibid.

page 36: "The furniture . . . and love." Ibid, p. 26.

page 38: "I am . . . the people." Chisholm, "Brooklyn Announcement."

"who dared . . . of change." Chisholm, "Excerpts from the National Visionary Leadership Project."

back cover: "I ran . . . been true." Chisholm, *The Good Fight*, p. 3.

PHOTOGRAPH CREDITS

Shirley St. Hill yearbook picture and campaign button: Shirley Chisholm '72 Collection, Archives & Special Collections, Brooklyn College Library

Shirley Chisholm and Conrad Chisholm: Bettmann

Shirley Chisholm taking oath of office: AP Photo/File

Shirley Chisholm opening presidential campaign: AP Photo/Bill Chaplis, File

Shirley Chisholm and Rev. Jesse Jackson: AP Photo/Joe Holloway Jr.

Shirley Chisholm and Barbara Lee: Courtesy of Congresswoman Barbara Lee

Entrance to Shirley Chisholm State Park: AP Photo/Julia Weeks

AUTHOR'S SOURCES

Barron, James. "Shirley Chisholm, 'Unbossed' Pioneer in Congress, Is Dead at 80." *New York Times* obituary, January 3, 2005: A00001.

Chisholm '72: Unbought & Unbossed. Directed by Shola Lynch. 20th Century Fox (DVD), released January 18, 2004.

Chisholm, Shirley. *The Good Fight*. New York: Harper & Row, 1973.

———. *Unbought and Unbossed*. Boston: Houghton Mifflin, 1970; 40th Anniversary Edition, Washington, DC: Take Root Media, 2010.

———. "Vote Chisholm 72: Brooklyn Announcement." January 25, 1973. http://www.4president.org/speeches/shirleychisholm1972announcement.htm.

Cosby, Dr. Camille O. "Excerpts from the National Visionary Leadership Project: Interview with Shirley Chisholm." Iowa State University, Archives of Women's Political Communication, May 7, 2002. https://awpc.cattcenter.iastate.edu/2017/03/09/excerpts-from-the-national-visionary-leadership-project-may-7-2002/.

Gutgold, Nichola D. *Paving the Way for Madam President*. Lanham, MD: Lexington Books/Rowman & Littlefield, 2006.

Jones, Robert. "The Audacity of Shirley Chisholm." *Brooklyn College Magazine* 1, no. 1 (Spring 2012): 11–15.

Leef, Deborah. "Shirley Chisholm/Barbara Jordan Forum." Transcript, 2005. https://www.jfklibrary.org/~/media/assets/Education%20and%20Public%20Programs/Forum%20Transcripts/2006/2006%2007%2028%20A%20Tribute%20to%20Shirley%20Chisholm%20and%20Barbara%20Jordan.pdf.

Little, Becky. "'Unbought and Unbossed': Why Shirley Chisholm Ran for President." History, December 8, 2014. https://www.history.com/news/shirley-chisholm-presidential-campaign-george-wallace.

Pollack, Jill S. *Shirley Chisholm*. New York: Franklin Watts, 1994.

The Shirley Chisholm Project: Brooklyn Women's Activism from 1945 to the Present. CUNY Brooklyn College archive. http://chisholmproject.com.

Winslow, Barbara. *Shirley Chisholm: Catalyst for Change*. Boulder, CO: Westview Press, 2014.